DOOMED HISTORY

T0012336

RADIATION DISASTER!

Chernobyl, 1986

by Nancy Dickmann

BEARPORT
PUBLISHING

Minneapolis, Minnesota

Credits: Front Cover, ©zefart/Shutterstock; 1, ©UPI/Alamy 3, © SvedOliver/Shutterstock; 4–5, ©Ruslan Mariborodin/Shutterstock; 6–7, ©muph/Shutterstock; 8, ©Parilov/Shutterstock; 9, ©Forgem/Shutterstock; 10, ©CE85/Shutterstock; 11, ©Nordroden/Shutterstock; 12–13, ©UPI/Alamy; 14, ©Ihor Khomych/Shutterstock; 15, ©Henrique NDR Martins/iStock; 16, ©Floreskuu/Shutterstock; 17, ©YekaterinaK/Shutterstock; 18, ©UPI/Alamy; 19, ©EnolaBrain81/Shutterstock; 20, ©Stefan Holm/Shutterstock; 21, ©andreac77/Shutterstock; 22, ©Images SPOT/Public Domain; 23, ©srulik/Shutterstock; 24, ©F Lamiot et A Villain/Public Domain; 25, ©Luigi Ottani/Shutterstock; 26, ©Sergii. Blinov/Shutterstock; 27, ©Hanna_Hanna/Shutterstock; 28, ©magiclab/Shutterstock; 29, ©LM Spencer/Shutterstock.

Bearport Publishing Company Product Development Team
President: Jen Jenson; Director of Product Development: Spencer Brinker; Senior Editor: Allison Juda; Editor: Charly Haley; Associate Editor: Naomi Reich; Senior Designer: Colin O'Dea; Associate Designer: Elena Klinkner; Associate Designer: Kayla Eggert; Product Development Assistant: Anita Stasson

Brown Bear Books
Children's Publisher: Anne O'Daly; Design Manager: Keith Davis; Picture Manager: Sophie Mortimer

Library of Congress Cataloging-in-Publication Data is available at www.loc.gov or upon request from the publisher.

ISBN: 979-8-88509-393-4 (hardcover)
ISBN: 979-8-88509-515-0 (paperback)
ISBN: 979-8-88509-630-0 (ebook)

For more information, write to Bearport Publishing, 5357 Penn Avenue South, Minneapolis, MN 55419.

CONTENTS

A NUCLEAR NEIGHBOR

The sun was shining on a spring day in Pripyat. The town's residents had no idea that soon, their lives would change forever.

Pripyat was a town in northern Ukraine. At the time it was part of the **Soviet Union**. Pripyat had been built for people who worked at the nearby Chernobyl **nuclear power** plant. The workers and their families lived in modern apartment buildings alongside schools, shops, gyms, and a hospital. They even had an amusement park.

Pripyat was founded in 1970. By 1986, nearly 50,000 people lived there.

Safety First?

Chernobyl was about 2 miles (3.2 km) southeast of Pripyat and was one of many nuclear power plants in the Soviet Union. In February 1986, a magazine had printed an article in which a government official boasted that the odds of a **meltdown** were 1 in 10,000 years. But the following month, a manager at Chernobyl warned that the plant was not as safe as the government claimed. A month later, she would be proven right.

THE FIRST SIGNS OF TROUBLE

The workers at Chernobyl had run safety checks in the past. Little did they know their next test would cause a deadly disaster.

The Chernobyl plant had four **reactors**, each of which produced a lot of heat. A system of pumps pushed water through the reactors to keep them cool. But this system ran on electricity, so if there was a power failure, the pumps would stop. The plant had backup **generators** for safety, but they would take more than a minute to start. That delay could cause a reactor to overheat.

Nuclear reactors are huge, complicated pieces of machinery housed in large buildings.

A reactor's turbine is like a huge fan with many blades. It spins when steam rushes past it.

A New Idea

Engineers thought they had a solution that could stop a disaster. Each reactor had a giant fan called a **turbine**. If there were ever a power failure, it would take the turbine a while to stop. This continued spinning could generate enough electricity to run the cooling pumps. In April 1986, the engineers at Chernobyl decided to try out their idea. Since Reactor 4 was going to be temporarily shut down for maintenance, this was the perfect opportunity for the test.

HOW A NUCLEAR REACTOR WORKS

A nuclear reaction happens when tiny **atoms** of a metal called **uranium** are split. This releases lots of energy. Extra **neutrons** released during the reaction cause other reactions that release even more energy.

Inside a nuclear reactor, uranium is packed into metal tubes called **control rods**. These rods absorb extra neutrons to control the speed of reactions in the reactor's **core**. As water flows past the tubes, it turns into steam, which spins the blades of the turbine. Then, a generator uses the spinning movement to make electricity.

More control rods in a reactor's core mean a slower nuclear reaction, less heat, and less electricity produced.

These nuclear cooling towers safely reduce heat when water flows through them.

The Night Shift

At 1:00 a.m., on April 25, Reactor 4 began the long process of powering down. But shortly after, another energy plant in the area unexpectedly lost power. Chernobyl needed to provide extra electricity, so the reactor test had to be delayed for several hours. By the time the workers received permission to proceed with the test, it was late and the night shift was on duty. These workers were not properly trained to run the test.

From the control room, engineers could raise and lower control rods to speed up or slow down the reaction.

Starting the Test

In the control room, the night shift leader, Aleksandr Akimov, was overseeing the shutdown and test. Reactor 4 could produce 3,200 **megawatts** (MW) of power, but the test only needed between 700 and 1,000 MW. By 12:05 a.m., on April 26, the reactor was producing 720 MW. But for some reason the power kept dropping further. Suddenly, at 12:28 a.m., it plummeted to just 30 MW. At this level, the reactor was unstable and in danger of overheating.

Change of Plans

Akimov wanted to cancel the test, but Anatoly Dyatlov, the deputy chief engineer, ordered it to continue. They raised control rods out of the reactor core to increase power, and about 30 minutes later the reactor had leveled out at 200 MW. This wasn't enough power to safely cool the core, but Dyatlov pushed ahead anyway. Suddenly, at 1:23 a.m. the power surged. Akimov pressed an emergency button to lower all the control rods and slow the nuclear reaction. But it didn't work. The rods jammed on their way into the core.

These blocks in the reactor are very heavy, yet during the test, one person said he saw them jumping.

DISASTER STRIKES

Something had gone terribly wrong, and the reactor was overheating. Moments later, it exploded.

The reactor's power output had jumped to about 30,000 MW—nearly 10 times its maximum capacity. It was putting out a huge amount of heat, instantly boiling its water into steam. The steam expanded quickly, causing a huge explosion inside the reactor.

WITNESS TO DISASTER

Aleksandr Yuvchenko was working the night of the explosion. He described the scene. "What we saw was terrifying. Everything that could be destroyed had been. . . . The right-hand side of the reactor hall had been completely destroyed, and, on the left, the pipes were just hanging. . . Everything around them was **rubble**."

Fireball

The explosion caused a fireball to erupt into the night sky. The air filled with dust and chunks of the reactor core. This **debris** was extremely hot and started fires everywhere it landed. But the real danger was invisible—the explosion had released huge amounts of deadly **radiation**.

The reactor was covered by a heavy roof that weighed more than 1,000 tons (900,000 kg). The explosion blew it right off.

Chunks of the reactor core like this had turned red hot. One firefighter picked one up and burned his hand.

Emergency Response

Just five minutes later, the first firefighters arrived at the power plant. They had been trained to fight fires, not to face nuclear disasters. They didn't have the right equipment to protect themselves from radiation. Some of the firefighters may not have understood how dangerous this job would be. Others may have known but continued out of a sense of duty.

On the Roof

Debris flying from the explosion caused fires to spark on the roof of the nearby Reactor 3. Some firefighters dealt with the blazes on the ground, and others went to tackle those on the roof. While they put out several small fires, their bodies were being bombarded by radiation. By about 2:30 a.m., the firefighters started vomiting and several of them collapsed.

Several firefighters died after being exposed to radiation at Chernobyl.

At the time of the explosion, construction crews were building two more reactors. Those reactors were never completed.

Shutting Down

Reactor 4 and neighboring Reactor 3 were shut down for safety. The firefighters continued to work, and by about 6:35 a.m., only the **inferno** raging in the core of Reactor 4 still burned. But this was the most dangerous fire. The longer it burned, the more radiation it released.

People in Pripyat listened to the radio for news while the disaster was happening.

The View from Pripyat

Officials had locked down Pripyat, so no cars were allowed to enter or leave the town. Residents could see the fire burning in the distance, but most didn't realize how dangerous it was.

WATCHING THE FIRE

Nadezhda Vygovskaya described watching the fire from Pripyat. "It was like the reactor was glowing. This wasn't any ordinary fire, it was some sort of shining. It was pretty. . . . People came from all around on their cars and their bikes to have a look. We didn't know that death could be so beautiful. . . . My throat tickled, and tears came to my eyes."

LIFE OR DEATH

As the sun came up on April 27, the reactor was still burning and pumping out huge amounts of deadly radiation.

At about 10:00 a.m. on the day after the explosion, helicopters began flying over the reactor, dumping a mixture of sand, clay, lead, and boron onto the blaze. They hoped to slow the radiation leak.

The helicopter pilots were exposed to radiation each time they flew over the reactor.

Time to Go

Despite the work of the brave pilots and firefighters, radiation levels remained too high. Officials finally decided to send buses to help the residents of Pripyat **evacuate**. At the time, people were told that they would have to stay away for only a few days. In reality, they were never allowed to return.

People couldn't take much with them. They had to leave most of their belongings behind.

RADIATION

Radiation is energy moving from one place to another. Most types are harmless. Lightbulbs, cell phones, and microwaves all give off safe levels of radiation. But high-energy radiation passes through a person's body and changes the atoms within it, which can damage skin and organs. It can also lead to cancer and even death.

The World Finds Out

At first, the Soviet government had kept the nuclear accident quiet. No one outside the Soviet Union—and very few people inside it— knew about the disaster. But on the morning of April 28, an alarm went off at a nuclear power plant in Sweden, nearly 700 miles (1,100 km) away. At first, the workers there thought they had a leak. But tests revealed that **radioactive** material from the Soviet Union had been carried to Sweden by the wind.

Telling the Truth

The Swedish government contacted the Soviet Union to find out what happened. The Soviet government was forced to admit that there had been an explosion and fire at Chernobyl. That night, Soviet news made a short TV announcement about the accident, making it sound like a small, contained event. But the explosion wasn't just a Soviet problem anymore—dangerous radiation was now reaching other countries.

Sheep in the United Kingdom, 1,500 miles (2,400 km) away, had so much radiation in their bodies that their meat could not be sold.

Stopping the Leak

Meanwhile, workers at Chernobyl were frantically trying to control the radiation leak and fight the fire that was still burning. Temperatures in the reactor had reached 2,200 degrees Fahrenheit (1,200 degrees Celsius). A fire that hot can't be put out by spraying water, so helicopters continued to try and smother it from above by dumping sand, clay, and lead onto the blaze. It took about 1,800 flights over a 10-day period to put out the fire. The amount of radiation being released finally began to drop.

Satellites gave the rest of the world the first images of the disaster, showing the roofless reactor still glowing and smoking.

Out at Last

Although the fire was out, the nuclear fuel and core debris inside the reactor were still extremely hot. They started to burn through the floor of the reactor, creating a kind of radioactive lava. If this burned down to the **water table** below the reactor, that water could boil and cause another explosion. To prevent this, workers started pumping super-cold liquid nitrogen under the reactor. Then, they decided to dig a tunnel beneath the reactor to install a cooling system.

WHAT HAPPENED NEXT

The fire was finally out, but the damage it caused would take decades to clean up.

The Soviet government called in hundreds of thousands of people to help with the clean-up. These people were known as liquidators. Some came from the military, but others were **civilians** who were asked to come or who volunteered to help. Some worked at the plant itself, while many more worked in the surrounding area.

The liquidators received medals for their work and are now treated like military veterans.

A Dangerous Job

One of the most dangerous jobs was clearing debris from the roof of Reactor 3. The radiation there was still so high that it made remote-controlled robots break down, so people were used instead. To avoid radiation sickness, each liquidator could stay on the roof for only about a minute, shoveling up as much debris as they could before rushing away.

UNPREPARED

Oleg Veklenko worked as a liquidator in May 1986. He said, "The recruitment offices called people up to go to Chernobyl. . . . They were not properly prepared or given special training. . . . They didn't realize the danger they were exposed to. At least myself and those with me weren't aware of it."

Cleaning the Land

The land around Chernobyl was now **contaminated** with radiation, and no one would be able to live there again. Liquidators cut down trees and bulldozed the land, clearing away the top layer of contaminated soil. They also built systems for filtering the radioactive water. Through this work, the liquidators were exposed to high levels of radiation and many suffered long-term health problems because of it.

Sealing It Off

Reactor 4 was still highly radioactive, so something needed to be done to cover and contain it. In May, workers started building a concrete casing that would help stop the radioactive material from leaking and spreading beyond the damaged reactor. To keep workers safe, a lot of the construction was done by robots. It wasn't possible to completely seal the reactor, but most of the radiation was contained by November.

The people from Pripyat needed a place to live, so a new town called Slavutych was built about 30 miles (50 km) away.

A New Solution

By 1987, Chernobyl's other three reactors were operating again, but it soon became clear that the damaged reactor's concrete casing would not last. High levels of radiation from inside had already damaged it. As a result, the entire power plant was finally shut down in 2000. In 2010, engineers from across Europe began working together to build a huge metal arch to cover Reactor 4.

The new structure, finished in 2019, weighs 33,000 tons (30 million kg) and should prevent radiation leaks for 100 years.

It is considered safe to make short visits to Pripyat. The town has become popular with tourists.

Chernobyl Today

Chernobyl is still part of an **exclusion zone** that covers about 1,000 square miles (2,600 sq. km). People aren't allowed to live there, but they can visit for very short periods. Radiation from the disaster is still found in plants and animals across Europe. Some populations in eastern Europe have higher rates of cancer, likely caused by the radiation. Scientists say it will be anywhere from 300 to 20,000 years before people can safely live in the Chernobyl area again.

KEY DATES

1977

September 26 The Chernobyl Nuclear Power Plant begins operation.

1986

April 25 Reactor 4 starts to power down for a safety test.

April 26

1:23 a.m. There is a surge in power, and the reactor explodes.

1:28 a.m. The first firefighters arrive at the scene.

2:15 a.m. The town of Pripyat is locked down.

6:35 a.m. All fires are out except the one in the core of Reactor 4.

April 27

10:00 a.m. Helicopters start dumping sand, clay, and lead into the reactor.

2:00 p.m. The evacuation of Pripyat begins.

April 28 A nuclear power plant in Sweden detects radioactive materials.

May 6 The fire in the reactor core is finally out.

November Work on the damaged reactor's concrete casing is finished.

2019

July Work on the new containment structure is finished.

QUIZ How much have you learned about the Chernobyl disaster? It's time to test your knowledge! Then, check your answers on page 32.

1. **Which reactor at Chernobyl was destroyed by an explosion?**
   a) Reactor 2
   b) Reactor 1
   c) Reactor 4

2. **Why were engineers running a safety test that night?**
   a) to see if a turbine could run the cooling pumps
   b) to test radiation levels
   c) to see if the reactor could produce even more power

3. **Which of these did helicopters dump onto the damaged reactor?**
   a) water and foam
   b) sand, clay, and lead
   c) dirt and liquid nitrogen

4. **Where did people outside the Soviet Union first realize something had gone wrong?**
   a) an army base in Poland
   b) a newspaper office in Germany
   c) a nuclear power plant in Sweden

5. **What name was given to the people who helped with the cleanup operation?**
   a) liquidators
   b) janitors
   c) scrubbers

GLOSSARY

atoms the tiny building blocks that make up all matter

civilians people who are not members of the military

contaminated made dirty, polluted, or poisonous

control rods tubes made from substances that slow down a nuclear reaction, leading to lower temperatures and less energy produced

core the center or middle part of something

debris broken pieces of a structure

evacuate to leave a dangerous place

exclusion zone an area that people aren't allowed to live in and where they must have special permission to enter

generators machines that produce electrical power

inferno a large fire

megawatts a unit of power

meltdown an accident in which radioactive nuclear fuel overheats and leaks out of the reactor

neutrons very small particles found in the center of an atom

nuclear power a way of generating electricity by using the energy released when atoms split

radiation energy traveling in waves; some types of high-energy radiation are very harmful

radioactive giving off harmful radiation

reactors machines in which atoms are split to release energy

rubble rough fragments of exploded stone, concrete, brick, or other material

Soviet Union a former country that was centered around Russia and had a communist government

turbine a large fan that spins when air or water flows past it

uranium a radioactive metal

water table a water-soaked layer of earth underneath the top layers of soil

INDEX

READ MORE

Kortemeier, Todd. *Chernobyl (Engineering Disasters).* Minneapolis: Abdo Publishing, 2020.

Twiddy, Robin. *Nuclear Nightmare! (Polluted Planet).* New York: Gareth Stevens Publishing, 2020.

Vonder Brink, Tracy. *Nuclear Power (Energy Sources).* New York: Crabtree Publishing, 2023.

LEARN MORE ONLINE

1. Go to **www.factsurfer.com** or scan the QR code below.

2. Enter **"Radiation Disaster"** into the search box.

3. Click on the cover of this book to see a list of websites.

Answers to the quiz on page 30

1) C; 2) A; 3) B; 4) C; 5) A

DOOMED HISTORY

RADIATION DISASTER!

Chernobyl, 1986

On the morning of April 26, 1986, an explosion at the Chernobyl nuclear power plant sent people scrambling. And this was only the beginning of the radiation disaster. Find out more about this doomed history.

Read all the books in this series:

For more *Doomed History* titles, visit our website.

BEARPORT
PUBLISHING

BearportPublishing.com

ISBN-13: 979-8-88509-515-0

90000

9 798885 095150

HAUNTED HISTORY

CAN'T REST IN PEACE

BY
LEAH KAMINSKI

BEAR CLAW